COLOR THRU HISTORY

The People of the Middle Ages
Elementary Supplement

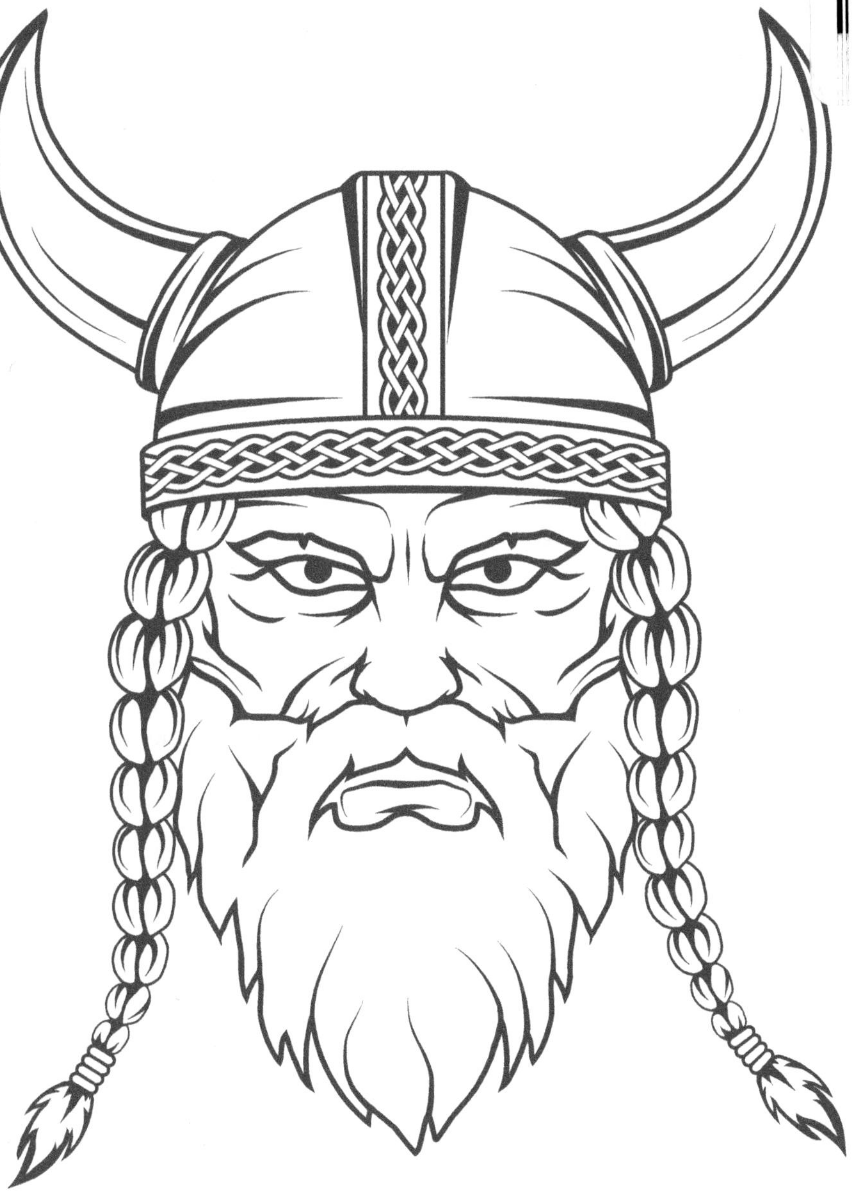

Fulton, KY

Current and upcoming titles:

Learn and Color Nature Series
- Medicinal Herbs
- Freshwater Fish
- Garden Edibles
- Reptiles

Learn and Color Stained Glass Series
- Landscapes & Seascapes
- Fish & Fowl
- Flowers

- Early Civilization
- The Ancient World
- The Middle Ages
- The Renaissance and Reformation
- The Industrial Revolution
- The Modern Age
- The Computer Age

Color Thru History™ – The People of the Middle Ages Elementary Supplement
© 2020 Master Design Marketing, LLC

All rights reserved. This book or parts thereof may not be reproduced in any form, stored in any retrieval system, or transmitted in any form by any means—electronic, mechanical, photocopy, recording, or otherwise—without prior written permission of the publisher, except as provided by United States of America copyright law or as noted below. For permission requests, write to the publisher, at "Permissions Coordinator," at the address below.

Learn & Color Books
 an imprint of Master Design Marketing, LLC
 789 State Route 94 E
 Fulton, KY 42041
 www.LearnAndColor.com

Permission is granted to make as many photocopies as you need for your own immediate family's homeschool use. All other use is strictly prohibited. Co-ops and schools may NOT photocopy any portion of this book. Educators must purchase one book for each student.

For information about special discounts available for bulk purchases, sales promotions, fund-raising and educational needs, contact Learn & Color Books at sales@LearnAndColor.com.

ISBN: 978-1-947482-26-5
Cover and interior design by Faithe F Thomas
Research by Caitlyn F Williams
Some images are © Faithe F Thomas
All other Images © DepositPhotos.com
Text in this book is a derivative of information by Wikipedia.com, used under CC BY 4.0.
The text of this book is licensed under CC BY 4.0 by Faithe F Thomas.
Look for the Scottish Flag somewhere in each of our books.

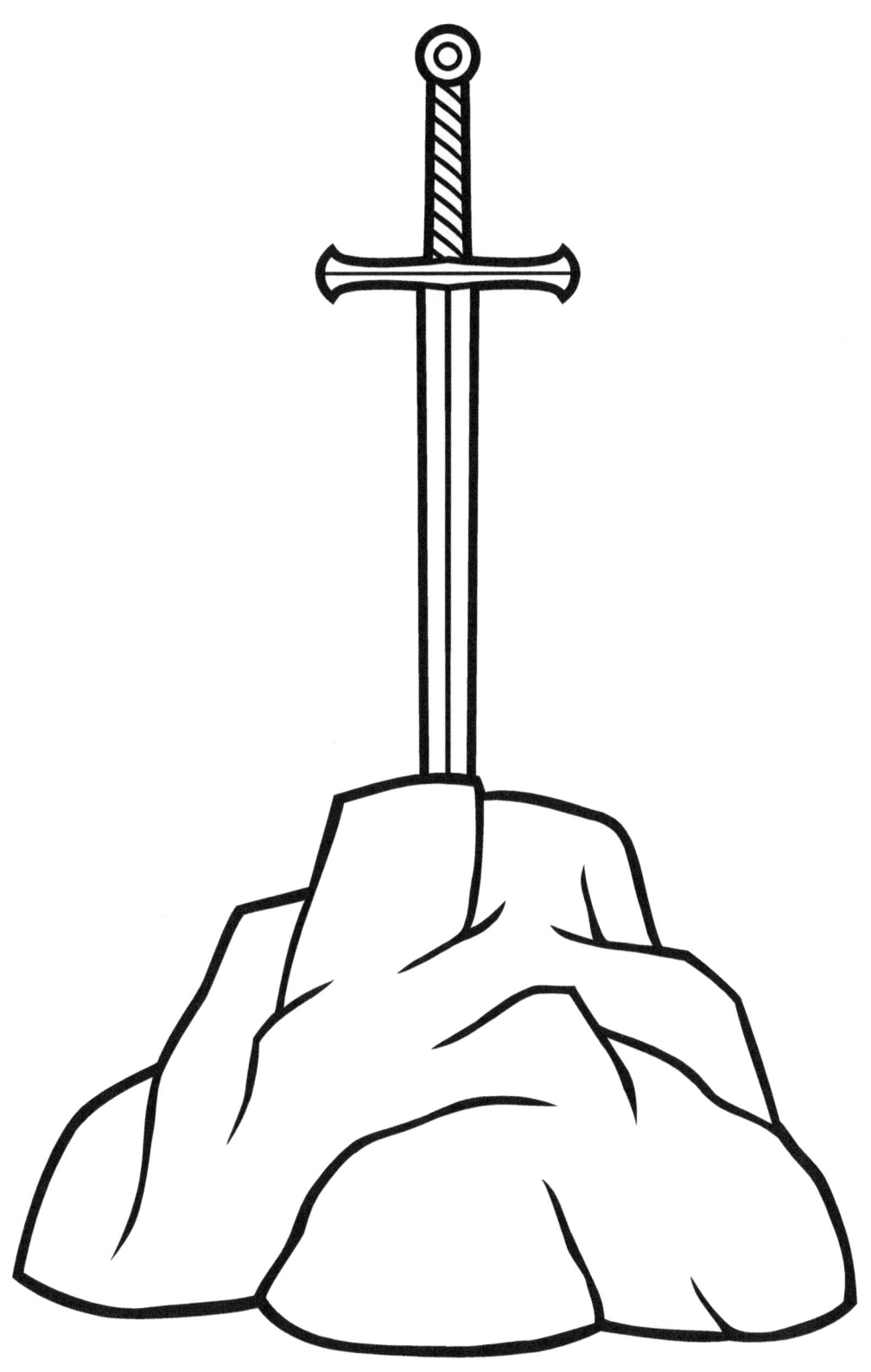

King Arthur was a legendary British leader who fought the Saxons.
He used his sword, which he pulled from a rock.

Clovis I was the first king of the Franks.
He became Catholic, which caused many of the Frankish people
to become Catholic as well.

King Æthelbert I of Kent was the first English king to convert to Christianity. He gave land to build churches.

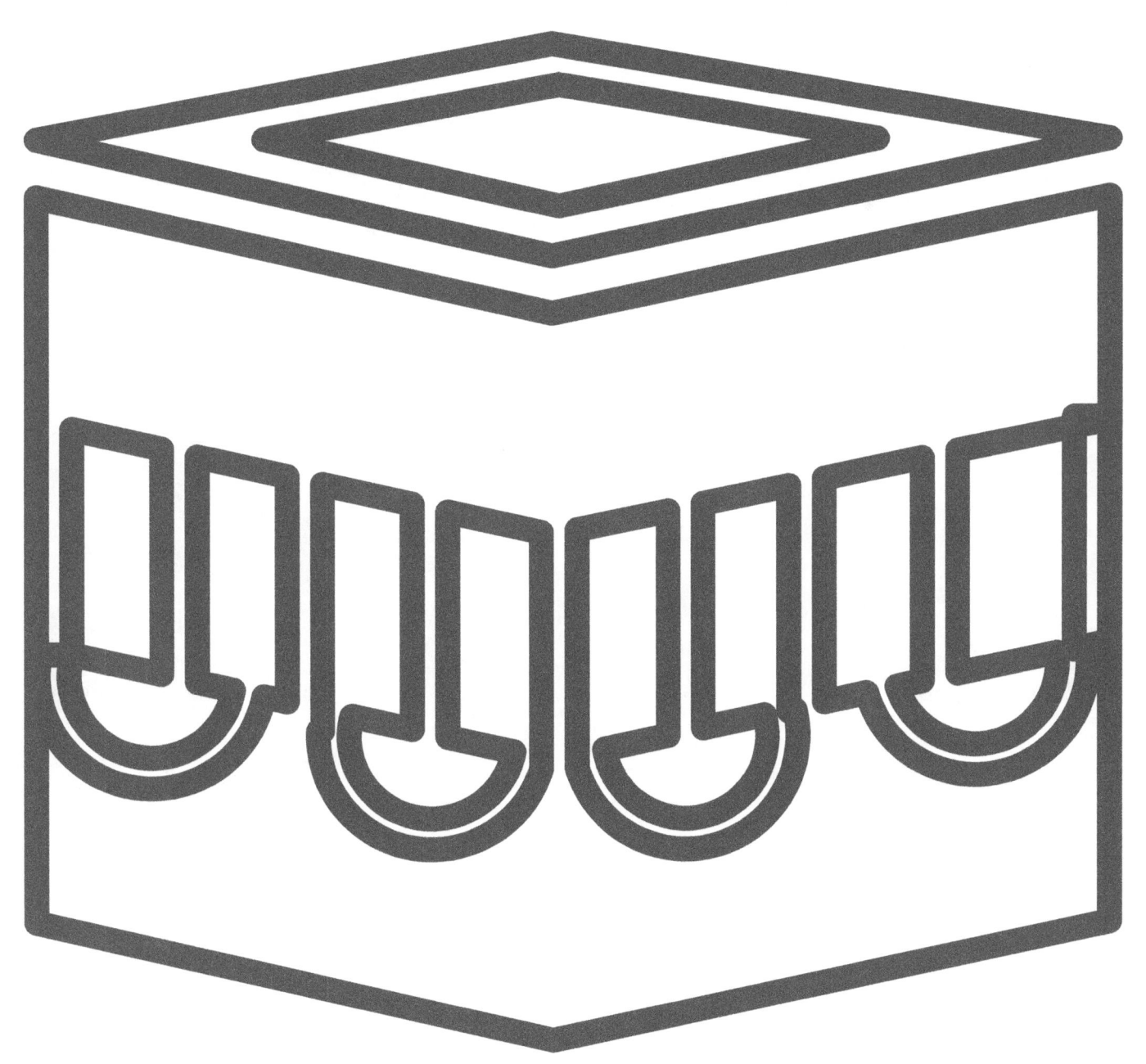

Muhammad was the founder of Islam.
The followers of Islam, called Muslims,
worship at a large black cube. It is covered with cloth.

Bede was a well known author, teacher, and scholar.
He wrote a book called the *Ecclesiastical History of the English People*.
He also tried to figure out the dates for Easter.

Charlemagne was king of the Franks. He has been called the "Father of Europe" because he united most of Western Europe for the first time since the Romans ruled.

Muhammad ibn Musa al-Khwarizmi was a Persian scholar who loved mathematics, astronomy, and geography. He is the "father of algebra." The word algorithm comes from his name.

Alfred the Great was a king in England. He is known for his laws, which were based on the laws in the Bible.

Erik the Red was a Norse explorer.
He founded the first settlement in Greenland.
He probably had red hair and a red beard.

Leif Erikson was the son of Erik the Red. He was the first known European to set foot on continental North America. He converted to Christianity and became a preacher in Greenland.

William the Conqueror was king of England.
While he was king, they build many castles.

El Cid was a military leader in medieval Spain.
He was a great soldier. After he died, many people wrote
stories and poems about him.

Hildegard of Bingen was a German Benedictine abbess, writer, composer, philosopher, Christian mystic, visionary, and polymath. She is considered to be the founder of scientific natural history in Germany.

Thomas Becket was Archbishop of Canterbury.
He argued with Henry II, King of England,
over the rights and privileges of the Church.

Henry II was king of England.
He created a genuinely English monarchy and,
ultimately, a unified Britain.

Saladin was the first sultan of Egypt and Syria.
He led the Muslim military campaign against the Crusaders.
His army defeated the Crusaders.

Richard the Lionheart was king of England at the time of the Crusades. He led in battle against Saladin. He won many times, but never defeated Saladin.

Genghis Khan was the founder of the Mongol Empire.
He established the Silk Road, which brought trade between
Northeast Asia, Muslim Southwest Asia, and Christian Europe.

Saint Francis of Assisi was an Italian Catholic friar, deacon, and preacher. He had a great love for animals. He is often remembered as the patron saint of animals.

Kublai Khan was the grandson of Genghis Khan.
He ruled the Mongol Empire.

Thomas Aquinas was a teacher and author of Christian thought.
He also wrote hymns.

Marco Polo was an Italian merchant, explorer, and writer, born in the Republic of Venice. He traveled from Europe to China. He wrote a book about his travels.

Osman I was the leader of the Ottoman Turks and the founder of the Ottoman dynasty.

Dante was a major Italian poet.
His writings helped inspire Western Art.

Sir William Wallace was a Scottish knight who became one of the main leaders during the First War of Scottish Independence.

William Tell was a Swiss mountain climber and an expert shot with the crossbow. He was able to shoot an apple off the head of his son Walter in a single attempt.

John Wycliffe was a theologian, reformer, English priest, and a seminary professor at the University of Oxford. He translated the Bible from Latin into Middle English – a version now known as Wycliffe's Bible.

Timur (Tamerlane) was the most powerful ruler in the Muslim world. He ruled over Persia and Central Asia.

Geoffrey Chaucer was the greatest English poet of the Middle Ages, best known for *The Canterbury Tales*.
He is often called the "father of English literature."

John Hus was a Czech theologian and dean of the Charles University in Prague. After John Wycliffe, Hus is considered the first church reformer.

www.ingramcontent.com/pod-product-compliance
Lightning Source LLC
Chambersburg PA
CBHW081203020426
42333CB00020B/2612